Network Firewall Security

Auditing Firewalls

Module 1:

Understanding Firewalls

Firewall Architecture Overview

What is firewall?

- A firewall is a security policy enforcement point that regulates access between computer networks
- Filters are inherently insecure services
- Controls TCP protocols
  -http, smtp, ftp, telnet etc
- Only one of many different security tool's to control and regulate network traffic

What do Firewalls Protocol?

- Data
- Proprietary corporate information
- Financial information
- Sensitive employee or customer data
- Resources
 - Computing resources

- Time resources
- Reputation
  - Loss of confidence in an organization
  - Intruder uses an organization's network to attack other sites

Who do Firewalls Guard Against?

- Internal Users
- Hackers
- Corporate Espionage
- Terrorist
- Common Thieves

Basic Firewall Components

- Policy
- Advanced authentication
- Packet inspection
- Application gateways

Common Internet Threats

- Denial of service attacks
  - Specific attacks that can cause a server crash
  - Flooding the server with traffic to dispute or deny service
- Intrusion threats

- Attacks on services/exploits
- The backend server may not be hardened enough for adequate protection, but the firewall can block external attacks
- Information threats
- "Viral" threats
- Defacement

How Vulnerable are Internet Services?

- E-mail or smtp – Simple Mail Transfer Protocol
- TCP/IP based port 25 (POP 110)
- Risks Include
- E-mail bombing (stalking)
- Anonymous harassment
- Large amounts of e-mail to a single user address
- Spamming
- Messages sent to numbers different users from a host
- Virus download mechanism
- Code Red
- Nimda
- Not always traceable
- POP and IMAP can be very insecure

How Vulnerable are Internet Services?

- FTP – File Transfer Protocol

- TCT/IP based port 20/21
- Risks Include
- Unencrypted authentication and data transfer
- Usernames and passwords can be "sniffed"
- Unencrypted data transfers
- Data can be viewed
- Often part of default installations
- Anonymous ftp is possible
- Privilege escalation

How Vulnerable are Internet Services?

- Telnet
- TCP/IP based port 23
- Risks include
- Unencrypted authentication
- Unencrypted interactive session
- Session hijacking
- Included in default installations
- Can allow remote root login

How Vulnerable are Internet Services?

- HTTP – Hypertext Transfer Protocol
- TCP/IP port 80
- Risks Include
- Browsers can be used to run dangerous commands

- Protocol can be used between user agents and other protocols i.e., smtp, nntp, ftp
- Difficult to secure
- Remote execution of commands and execution (server side)
- Nom-secure add-on applications
- Java
- Cookies
- Soap

How Vulnerable are Internet Services?

- HTTPS – Secure Hypertext Transfer Protocol
- TCP/IP based port 443
- Risks Include
- Browsers can be used to run dangerous commands
- Remote execution of commands and execution (server side)
- Becomes a tunnel for any data
- Can be used to subvert firewall/security controls

How Vulnerable are Internet Services?

- DNS
- TCP and UDP based ports 53 and 1024
- Risks include
- DNS cache poisoning

- Bad data to redirect valid connections to the wrong server
- DNS spoofing
- Bad data to redirect valid connections to the wrong server
- Absolutely needed for network services

How Vulnerable are Internet Services?

- SNMP – Simple Network Management Protocol
- UDP based
- Risk include
- Unencrypted data transfers
- Poor authentication through "community relationships"
- Transfer of highly sensitive data
- Does use access lists

How Vulnerable are Internet Services?

- NFS – Network File Systems
- NFS is a shared file structure
- Based on a trust model of network machines
- Certain machines can access shared file systems
- Risks include
- No "user" authentication
- IP Spoofing to gain access
- Most secure NFS is still very insecure

The "2002 Computer Security Institute/FBI Computer Crime and Security Survey" Reported:

- 90% of survey respondents (Primarily larger corporations) detected computer security breaches. Respondents reported a wide range of attacks:
- 44% detected system penetration from the outside
- 44% detected denial of service attacks
- 76% detected employee abuse of Internet access privileges
- 85% detected computer viruses, worms, etc.
- 80% acknowledged financial losses due to computer security breaches
- 44% were willing and/or able to quantify their financial losses (these losses were $455 million).
- Most serious losses occurred through theft of proprietary information and financial fraud.
- 74% cited their Internet connections as a frequent point of attack and 44% cited their internal systems ands frequent point of attack
- 34% reported intrusions to low enforcement (up from only 16% in 1996)

Firewall Architecture Overview

- Basic Firewall Components

- Software
- Hardware
- Purpose Built/Appliance based

Module 1:

Understanding Firewalls

Firewall Software Types

Firewall Software Types

- Problems to watch for
- Administrative limitations
- Access
- Monitoring
- Logging
- Management requirements
- Additional control points
- Additional non-secure applications required
- Software limitations
- Capacity
- Availability
- Hardware

Packet Filtering Firewalls

- Packet filtering one of the oldest, and one of the most common types of firewall technologies. Packet filters inspect each packet of information individually, examining the source and destination IP address and ports. This information is compared to access control rules decide whether the given packet should be allowed through firewall.

- Packet filters consider only the most basic attributes of each packet, and they don't need to remember anything about the traffic since each packet is examined in isolation. For this reason they can decide packet flow very quickly.
- Because every packet of every connection is checked against the access control rules, larger, complex rule bases decrease performance. And because packet filters can only check low-level attributes, they are not secure against malicious code hiding in the other layers. Packet filters are often used as a first defense in combination with other firewall technologies, and their most common implementation today is seen in the access control list of routers at the perimeters of networks.
- For simple protocols or one-sided connections, like ICMP or SNMP traps, it is still useful to use packet filtering technology.

Packet Filtering Firewalls

- Products
- Cisco Pix
- Typically routers
- First Generation Firewall Technology
- Fast but not very flexible
- Can be used as a first line of defense
- Application Level Firewalls
- Application level firewalls are the third firewall technology traditionally seen in the market. These firewalls, also known as application proxies, provide the most secure type of data connection because they can examine every layer of the communication, including the application data. To achieve this security proxies, as their name suggests, actually mediate connections. The connection from a client to server is intercepted by the proxy. If the proxy determines that the connection is allowed, it opens a second connection to the server from itself, on behalf of the original host. The data portion of each packet must be stripped off, examined, rebuilt, and sent again on the second connection.
- This through examination and handling of packets means that proxy firewalls are very secure and generally slow. Proxies are also limited as firewalls, because they must understand the application layer.

As new protocols are developed, new proxies must be written and implemented to handle them.

Application Level Firewalls

- Web Proxy Servers
- Application Proxy Servers
- Products
- None that are strictly Proxy based
- "Gateway Servers"
- Second Generation Firewall Technology
- Makes connections on behalf of the client
- Not flexible

Hybrid Firewalls

- Performs Packet Filtering functions
- Performs Application Proxy functions
- Third Generation Firewall Technology
- Products
- Raptor Firewall by Symantec
- Firewall 1 by Checkpoint
- Sidewinder Firewall by Secure Computing
- Lucent Brick by Lucent

Stateful Inspection ©

- Stateful inspection architecture utilizes a unique, patented INSPECT Engine which enforces the security policy on the gateway on which it resides. The INSPECT Engine looks at all communication layers and extracts only the relevant data, enabling highly efficient operation, support for a large number of protocols and applications, and easy extensibility to new applications and services.
- The INSPECT Engine is programmable Check Point's powerful INSPECT Language. This provides important system extensibility, allowing Check Point, as well as its technology partners and end-users, to incorporate new applications, services, and protocols, without requiring new software to be loaded. For most new applications, including most custom applications developed by end users, the communication-related to behavior of the new application can be incorporated simply by modifying one of Firewall- 1's built-in script templates via the graphical user interface. Even the most complex applications can be added quickly and easily via the INSPECT Language.

Stateful Inspection

- New technology incorporating
- Patented technology

- INSPECT engine
- Application Level Proxy
- Products
- Checkpoint NG (Exclusive)

Multi-Layer Inspection ©

- Multi-layer inspection is a packet and connection verification process developed by Stone soft to ensure maximum security without compromising systems throughput. Stone Gate's security policies determine when to use stateful connection tracking, packet filtering, or application-level security. The system expends the resources necessary for application-level security only when the situation demands it and without unnecessarily slowing or limiting network traffic.

Multi-Layer Inspection

- New technology incorporating
- Application proxies
- State Inspection
- Packet filtering
- Products
- Stone Gate by Stone soft (exclusive)

Firewall Software Types

- Be sure to understand what your customer is using
- Know your products
- Speaks to the firewall vendor for insight
- Compare responses of customer and vendor
- One firewall type or multiple types

Module 1:

Understating Firewalls

Firewall Hardware Types

Firewall Hardware Types

- Three basic hardware options
- Appliance based systems
- Purpose built
- Simple
- Highly integrated
- 3rd Party servers
- General use systems
- Additional support channel
- Greater flexibility
- Hybrid servers
- Purpose built for a limited product line
- Often closely integrated with software offerings
- May have separate support channel
- Most have highly integrated components

Firewall Hardware Types

- Appliance based system problems
- OS and Kernel hardening and security may be done by vendor only
- Tightly coupled software and hardware may have insecure code unknown to user
- Hard to inspect or verify
- All security controls are determine through a single vendor
- Appliances are used to simplify implementation and support effects causing some loss of administrative control

Firewall Hardware Types

- 3rd party server problems
- OS and Kernel hardening and security must be done by implementation staff
- Expertise
- Procedures
- OS software may have many known vulnerabilities/security holes
- Each must be plugged
- All security controls are determine through corporate policy
- Implementation difficulties

- Consistency challenges
- 3rd party systems require a larger degree of administration and procedure

Firewall Hardware Types

- Hybrid servers
- OS and Kernel hardening is started by vendor and completed by end user security staff-can help to make it more robust
- Packaged software and hardware are generally reviewed for security
- May or may not adhere to policy
- All security controls are determine through a more partnered structure
- Hybrid servers are also used to simplify implementation and support efforts without giving away administrative control

Module 1:

Understanding Firewalls

Network Firewall Architecture

Network Firewall Architecture

- Screening Router
- Simple Firewall

- Multi-Legged firewall
- Firewall Sandwich
- Layered Security Architecture

Screening Router

- Access Lists provide security
- Routers are application aware
- only inspects network level information
- Layer 3 of the OSI model
- Does not provide a great deal of security
- Very fast
- Not commonly used alone for security

Screening Router

Simple Firewall

- Small Companies with limited security needs
- Only utilizes two interfaces
- Trusted
- Un-trusted
- Provides modest security
- Does not offer dmz sandbox
- Inherently allows some level of connections between trusted and un-trusted networks

Simple Firewall

Multi-Legged Firewall

- Small to large sized business
- Security need is expanded
- Provides stronger security
- Creates a secure sandbox for semi-trusted services
- Flexible and secure

Multi-Legged Firewall

Firewall Sandwich

- Medium to large businesses
- Higher costs
- More serious need for security
- Provides a physical separation of networks
- Provides policy segregation between inside and outside firewalls
- Reduce administrative holes

Firewall Sandwich

Layered Firewall Approach

- Large enterprises with low risk tolerance
- Separates internal environments
- Reduces computer crimes
- Most attacks are internally based
- Deters malicious activities

- Controls overhead administrative traffic
- Allows IDS to work more effectively

Layered Firewall

Defense in depth

- Security has no single right answer
- Use every tool available to bolster security
- Layered security is always the best approach
- Strong security controls coupled with audit, administrative reviews, and an effective security response plans will provide a strong holistic defense

End of Module 1

Questions?

Network Firewall Security

Auditing Firewalls

Module 2:

Security Operations

Firewall Administration Overview

Firewall Administration Overview

- Administrative Access
- Break Fix Response

- Monitoring and Alarming
- Logging
- Policy/Rule set Administration

Module 2:

Security Operations

Administrative Access

Administrative Access

- What is Administrative Access?
- Administrative Access refers to a group's need to gain control over a system for the purpose of discharging their chartered duties. This access includes, but is not limited to: Monitoring, Log Analysis, Break fix support, User administration, Rule/Policy implementation, OS configuration, software/hardware implementation, and patch/upgrade implementation.
The need of any group to have this control should be carefully considered. Control rights delegated to teams should to clearly stated in your Corporate Security Policy.

Administrative Access

- Who might need access?
- Support Staff

- Implementation staff
- Design staff
- Network staff
- Audit or Review staff
- Many groups depending on your organizational structure

Administrative Access

- Types of access
- Read/View
- Typical need for design or Network staff
- Add
- Typical need for support and/or Implementation
- Change
- Typical needs for Support and/or Implementation
- Delete
- Typical needs for Support and/pr Implementation
- Audit/Over-site
- Typical for Audit or review teams

Administrative Access

- Software Access control
- Most systems are restrictive
- Role based access is often missing
- Inherent user rights of root/admin cause challenges

- Root/admit privilege is required to run firewall app
- Root privilege is same on IS and firewall
- Access to view often equals access to change or delete
- Elevation of privileges
- Organizational roles add complexity
- The have and have notes vs. need and function

Administrative Access

- Products to help provide control
- Many and diverse: sudo
- All have limitations
- Control commands
- Create separate user group from root
- Privilege can be upgraded inappropriately by user
- Most provide a patch and not the solution
- Firewall products need to incorporate the required control

Administrative Access

- Passwords
- Strong passwords
- Centralized administration
- De-centralized management in a large environment is trouble

- Two factor authentication
- Physical access
- Access points for administration a must
- Operation Center with strong physical controls

Module 2:

Security Operation

Break Fix response

Break Fix response

- Business units must have clear notification path
- Organizations must have clear response plan
- What teams perform support?
- What support level is each responsible for
- 1ST LEVEL
- 2ND LEVEL
- 3RD LEVEL
- What privileges do each of three team have

Break Fix response

- Talent
- Each group must be properly trained
- For every product they support
- Certifications
- General security knowledge

- Running firewalls and running them securely are different
- Procedurally
- How they discharge their responsibilities properly
- i.e. Allowable change
- break fix clearly define form change

Break Fix Response

- Vendor relationships and support
- Notification path clear to all team members
- Internal web site a good communication device
- Support contracts
- Up to date
- Inclusive of all products
- Repercussions of no support agreement
- Patch update access
- Security fix access

Break Fix Response

- Interaction with product owners
- Business units own application and are experts in the business need which typically conflicts with security policy/process
- Put in a change when fixing a problem

- Make change on the BU side that requires a firewall change that is insecure
- Without regard implement changes that break service and require firewall changes to restore production
- Re-IP a dB sever
- Change the communication protocol

Break Fix Response

- Oversight
- Does the fix change security
- Policies are done slowly with forethought
- Break fix is done fast and in a vacuum
- Does the fix change the design
- Updating design/risk matrixes
- Who is responsible
- How do we ensure it is done?

Module 2:

Security Operations

Monitoring and Alarming

Monitoring and Alarming

- Firewall Monitoring Problems
- OPSEC

- Greatly limits a groups ability to perform good monitoring
- Monitoring and communication fly in the face of "need to know" security concepts
- Products
- Geared toward functionality-not security
- Host Agents often open security holes
- Remote login access
- Random ports
- Root level access for tools
- Customer disclosure
- Customer want access to tools to track system performance
- Good monitoring often discloses sensitive information

Monitoring and Alarming

- Who performs monitoring?
- Requires access
- Discloses information
- Is access being delegated to other for any reason?
- Who has access?
- What controls are in place?
- What rights have they been delegated?
- What product is being used?
- Check for encryption and transport protocol

- Check loading and maintenance plans

Monitoring and Alarming

Module 2:

Security Operations

Logging

Logging

- Logging is very important
- Provides history of access
- Provides attack information
- Provides for Policy audit checking
- Provides trending analysis for capacity planning
- Provides evidence for events

Logging

- Firewall Logging Problems
- Many firewalls do not log effectively
- Extremely large files
- Different to manage and review
- Products have logs written to different files
- Access to many logs requires root access to firewalls
- Log analysis products are add-on and expansive
- Few organizations log effectively

Logging

- Logging Methods
- Local
- Directed to files (poor form a security perspective)
- Remote
- Syslog
- Udp protocol is not reliable or secure (new syslog is better)
- Cannot be used as evidence: not credible
- Separated management network
- Some products are managed and logged in isolated network
- Logging can be reliable and separate from firewall system
- Firewall products often account for good logging
- Ask good questions

Policy/Rule set Administration

- General security Policy Guidelines
- Least Privilege Concept
- Allow least amount of access to allow someone to complete their duties
- Government orange and red books
- Detailed security controls
- Great reference material

Policy/Rule set Administration

- General security Policy Guidelines
- Modems
- Very insecure
- Look for them on routers as a backup
- Remote vendor administration
- Banned by policy, allowed only be documented exceptions
- Protocols
- Tcp is the most easily controlled
- Session oriented
- Firewall compatible

Policy/Rule set Administration

- General security Policy Guidelines
- Protocols continued
- UDP
- Use an little as possible
- Needed for some require and some desired functions
- Monitoring, logging, snmp management
- Netbios
- Easily attacked
- Bad trust model

Policy/Rule set Administration

- General security Policy Guidelines
- Authentication
- Passwords
- Two factor
- Controls
- CA and digital certificates
- Encryption
- Data classification
- Strength
- Where/when

Policy/Rule set Administration

- General security Policy Guidelines
- Allowed services
- Should be known and highly controlled
- www
- http
- smtp
- vpn service
- dns
- Avoid inherently insecure service where possible
- Finger
- Telnet
- ftp
- nfs

- Remote admin tools (some have good controls others do not)

Network Firewall Security

Auditing Firewalls

Module 3:

Security Policy

Understanding Firewall Policies, Standards and Procedures

Why Conduct a Policy Audit

- The policy audit is the most difficult portion of a firewall audit
- The security policy is the single most important part of the firewall setup
- Security policy must be tied to the overall risk – vs. – cost benefit
- If your security policy does not account for backups, risk is not controlled.
- Today we will discuss a department audit (firewalls)

Policy Defined

- Policy

- The rules and regulations set by the organization. Policy determines the type of internal and external information resources employee can access, the kinds of programs they may install on their own computers as well as their authority for reserving network resources.
- Generally a security policy is a document that states in writing how a company plans to protect the company's physical and information technology assets. A security policy ii often considered to be a "living documents"
- Policy is typically general and set at a high level within the organization. Policies that contain details generally become too much of a "living document"

Standards

- Ensure that a products is fit for it's intended purposes and to ensure compatibility between computers
- Industry Standards
- For a Department audit, standards should exist between different business units and internally so that all team members understand how the different products work together

Procedure

- Established or prescribed methods to be followed routinely for the performance of designated operations or in designated situations – called also *standing operating procedure*

Example

- The policy may indicate what type of data or protocol must run through a firewall
- Standards will dictate the type of firewall
- Procedure will show how the day to day tasks ensure that the spirit of the policy is maintained
- Today we will use the term policy to include Policy, Standards, and Procedure

Overview of this Module

- Policy Minimums
- Access
- Break Fix Response
- Monitoring and Alarming
- Logging
- Policy/Rule Set Administration

Starting the Policy Audit

- Indentify who are the player
- Implementation, support, and design

- Wait to define scope until you understand the policy and players
- Does the division support the company's goals
- Does the department support the division policy
- Interaction with other groups (networks, IDS, Antivirus, business units,)

Identify Right Away

- Does the policy permit anything that's not explicitly prohibited, or does it prohibit everything that's not explicitly permitted
- Pros and Cons to each approach
- Depends on the corporate philosophy but either is acceptable; however, most will tend to be more restrictive

Identity Right Away

- Authority for policy
- Without authority no security policy can succeed
- Business units will always attempt to meet their needs, security is in their way
- Must have authority to make business follow the policy
- If they violate there must be consequences

Initial Items to Review

- Contingencies
- How many items must line up for the policy to be effective.
- Complexity
- Length of policies
- Part of overall organization risk management strategy
- You cannot do a firewall audit without familiarity of general security policy

Initial Items of Review

- Out of date
- Version control of the policy
- Approval process/Change management
- Who will own findings

Initial Items of Review

- Does policy innumerate the apps in use
- Does policy address the hardware/software, versions
- How is policy updates
- Can it react with the speed of new technology
- Define responsibility of tasks
- Overall controlling authority
- Internal audit controls
- Tools
- Oversights

- Process to update failed procedures
- Information sharing

Specific Necessary in Policy

- Policy should address
- Risk vs. cost trade off
- Sign off for exceptions
- Risk avoidance or informed acceptance
- Who policies / enforces the policy
- Role based admin
- Root password control
- How is access defined and controlled
- Password strength/resets grant access
- Reporting, alarming

Specific Necessary in Policy

- The groups that should be accounted for:
- Implementation
- Changes, new systems, removing, tracking changes, proper approval,
- Easiest to audit and everyone focuses on the most, spend the least amount of time here
- Design

- Approval, templates/format, traffic allowed, protocols, general defined guidelines, channel back to policy makers to get new changes
- Hardest, so many spend little time, should spend the most time

Specific Necessary in Policy

- Support
- Inventory control, response to issue, engage vendors, track issue, trend problems, access to designs,
- Almost equal to design, ok one day does not matter if someone makes a simple change to the system
- Hands on audit
- Others optional

Specific Necessary in Policy

- Sensitive data storage/transportation
- Rule sets
- System backup
- Logs
- Physical security of systems
- Good network security will not help if the firewall has unrestricted physical access
- On premises
- Off premises
- Transit

Module 3:

Security Policy

Policy as the Underpinnings of a Secure Infrastructure

Access Control Policy

- The box
- The software
- The connected storage devices
- Roles
- Controls
- Tools

Break Fix Response

- Controls to maintain system integrity
- Availability
- Response times
- Skills of available engineers
- Interaction with other groups
- Vendor
- Business units
- Support partners

Administration

- Security is a function of system administration

- System administration must be based in policy
- Tools
- System configuration checkers
- Build documents
- Allows for consistency
- Lists of installed software
- Location within file structure
- Permissions

Code

- Software/Hardware Vendors
- Patches/fixes
- New applications/OS upgrades
- Kernel changes
- Business Unit requests
- Application updates
- New applications
- Authentication changes
- Security updates/patches
- Sense of urgency/timelines
- Testing
- Procedures
- Not co-mingled with production environment

Policy to Ensure Security of the Code

- Why
- Most secure environments can be breached through a firewall accessible services
- Poor coding allows remote administrative access through common HTTP services
- Problems
- Buffer overflows
- Cross Site Scripting
- Mechanisms
- Code review
- Application firewall products
- Applications proxies

Infrastructure in Support of Policy

- Infrastructure allow you to meet policy requirements
- Once you know version check available resources for known issue and compare to the firewalls
- Engineering resources available
- Can they fulfill the policy requirements
- Training

Module 3:

Security Policy

Rule Base, Logging, Reporting

Monitoring

- What is required to be monitored in order to comply with policy
- Reporting
- Who has access to the data
- What tools are used to parse data
- Transportation of data
- Tools and protocols allowed
- If policy requires certain levels of data to be encrypted how is monitoring data transported
- SNMP (version 3 is encrypted) /Mail/UDP/TCP
- Alarming
- How
- To where

Logging

- Daily review at a minimum
- Tools are important, more reliable than a person and can be done constantly
- Done by someone with knowledge of what they are looking for
- Forensic analysis
- What is logged
- Successful attempts, failed?
- Where is the data stored

- Should be remote to server
- How is it transported

Response to Alerts

- Does the policy differentiate alerts
- Incident response (hacking)
- System problems
- Network problems
- Interaction with outside agencies
- Police
- Press
- Discloser of information
- Who/when

Rule Set Administration

Firewall rules are the heart of any firewall system. A mistake in the firewall rules can undermine all security controls.

- Who designs the changes
- Who approves the designs
- Are there standards to creating a design
- E-mail, FTP, Web
- Blocking Sites/Ports
- Who is authorized to change the rules
- Who reviews these changes

- Machines of making the change
- On the machine directly
- Staged
- Access points

Backup/Restore

- Media
- Tape
- Mainframe
- Another host
- Frequency of backups
- Consider the type of data
- Consider frequency of changes to the environment
- Restoration
- Contingencies for types of problems
- Hacking
- Loss of hardware
- Loss of network
- Loss of data center

Module 3:

Security Policy

Mapping Policy to the Firewall

Goals

- Match policy to the physical systems
- Match policy to team member processes
- Random sample of systems
- Review of system inventory
- System review
- Define Files to see
- Results of previous internal/external scans
- Penetration tests

Mechanics

- Interview
- Establish a rapport
- Down play your role
- Sympathize
- Discuss opportunities that audits can present
- Ask for "off the record" feedback about processes
- Look for opportunities to move in a new direction
- Identify others to interview
- Job shadow
- Is it difficult to do the work in compliance with policy
- Do short cuts results

Mechanics

- System review
- Define files to see

- Rule sets
- Password
- Operating system
- Software configuration
- Logs
- Must be archived elsewhere
- Define the manner in which you will have access

Pitfalls of too Much Policy

- Can't be followed
- Impedes implementation
- Costs too much to the organization
- Too restrictive for business
- Does not allow for risk (risk avoidance opposed to informed acceptance)

Module 3:

Security Policy

Understanding Firewall Policies, Standards and Procedures

Network Firewall Security

Auditing Firewalls

Module 4:

Understanding Firewalls

Building An Audit Plan

Overview of the Basic Steps

- Review the policy
- Get an organization chart
- Determine the abilities of the firewall
- What "add on" applications (e.g. IDS, anti-virus)
- Can it enforce the policy
- Does the design enforce the policy
- Identify the supporting components
- Log server
- Backup server
- Access points
- Review the configuration of the firewall
- Conduct spot tests

Firewall Review

- As you are auditing the implementation
- Build a list of:
- Software used (include versions)
- Don't forget the remote access software
- Don't forget any clients running on the users end
- Hardware
- Operating system

- Custom kernels

Research

- Check available online resources looking for known security holes
- Follow up with the manufacture to find out their recommendations for configuration/administration
- What are the newest versions and why are they not being utilized
- Watch for end of life products

Back to the Firewall

- Check to see if is susceptible to any of the known vulnerabilities
- Patches
- Mitigation controls
- Proceed to the "Detail Audit" and use of tools
- Run netstat to identify open ports
- Run LSOF = list of open files

Spot Checks

- Attempt to bypass various controls
- If an outbound only rule try to run the service inbound
- FTP
- Telnet

- If it is suppose to filter content, try to pass the content
- Ensure you have management approval, plan to do the work after business hours

Tools to Aid the Audit

- Be careful to trust in tools too much
- A lack of finding does not mean the system is set up well
- Use them to verify what you have already found out
- We are not doing a penetration test
- Firewalls have changed so fast that good comprehensive auditing tools have not been developed

Tools to Aid the Audit

- Port Scanner (nmap)
- Should re-enforce what you found from running netstat
- Security scanning tools should show little information
- Satan, Internet Scanner, work good to audit a trusted network for obvious issue but do not work well on a bastion hosted locked down OS
- Go to a class and be proficient

Detail Audit

- Access to the firewall should be authorized
  - How are employees and non employees given access
  - Obtain a list of uses on the firewall
  - Cross check with staff lists/organization chart
  - Remote Administration
- Onetime passwords
- Other secure methods
- Encrypted link
  - How is access changed or revoked
  - How is access reviewed
- Mechanics of authentication
- Frequency of review
- Password reset/changing passwords
- Root password control

Detail Audit

- Firewall should enforce security policy (encryption, viruses, URL blocks, proxy/packet filter types of traffic)
  - Obtain the rule set
  - How are rule sets stored to maintained to ensure that they have not been tampered with
  - Checksums regularly verified?
  - Is effectiveness of firewall rested

- Review processes running on firewall; are they appropriate
- Does the firewall provide adequate notice when an exploit it attempted?

Detail Audit

- Control
- Physical access to the firewall controlled
- How are software updates done
- Control of sensitive information
- IP addresses
- Access tied to an individual
- Control of hidden/system accounts
- Control of devices used to manage firewalls

Detail Audit

- Network configuration
- Obtain a design
- Does the firewall properly protect the DMZ
- Identify the monitoring and control of traffic procedures used
- NAT to protect internal address space
- Does firewall used dynamic or static address translation

Detail Audit

- Connections should be logged and monitored
  - What events are logged
- Inbound services
- Outbound services
- Access attempts that violate policy
  - How frequent are logs monitored
- Differentiate from automated and manual procedure
  - Alarming
- Security breach response
- Are the responsible parties experienced?
  - Monitoring of privileged accounts

Detail Audit

- Custom written scripts
  - Prolific in Unix environments
  - Should be listed, and reviewed
- Use of mail services

Detail Audit

  - Management Reports
  - Capacity
  - Incidents
  - Alerts
  - Trending

Detail Audit

- Changes to the firewall configuration
- How are they authorized
- How are they tested
- Safe environment
- Tracked
- Back out plan
- Staging of rules/review by a second party
- Change control vs. break fix
- Changes should be scheduled and approved
- Break fix should be limited to restore to working state without adding anything new
- Any new IP address, URL changes must be approved and cannot be addressed as break fix

Detail Audit

- Recovery
- Plan developed in compliance with business continuity requirements
- Are the time limits acceptable and achievable
- Frequency of testing
- Review the results of the most recent test

Resources

- www.bugtraq.com
- www.cert.org

- RFC 2096 Site Security Handbook
  For drafting security policies
- "firewalls and Internet Security" Repelling the Wily Hacker:, by Bill Cheswick and Steve Bellovin
- "Building Internet Firewalls." By Brent Chapman and Elizabeth Zwicky
- Current up to date information form mailing lists
- Bug Traq
- security Focus

Introducing Check Point Endpoint Security Single agent for endpoint security

Name

Title

Agenda

Endpoint security Solution

Overview

Endpoint Security Solution

- **Single agent Single Console** for Simplified Execution
- **Powerful Security** for Confident Protection

Agenda

Endpoint Security Solution

Security Challenges

Endpoint Security Challenges

Too many security agents to manage

Multiple admin consoles – a console for each agent

Software compatibility issue between separate agents

Resulting in…

Never enough security

Increased administration time and costs

Multiple test cycles – every time an agent in updated

1st Enterprise Endpoint Security Solution

Check Point

Single Agent for Endpoint Security

Firewall/NAC Antivirus anti-spyware Data Security Remote Access

- Mitigates the broadest range of endpoint risks
- Unifies all essential components
- Only solution that includes both data security and remote access

Agenda

Endpoint Security Solution

Single Agent, Single Console

Single Agent for Endpoint Security

Easy to Deploy and Manage

- Only comprehensive endpoint security solution:
- Firewall, NAC & Program Control
- Antivirus and anti-spyware
- Data security
- Remote Access
- Single installation
- Single, intuitive interface
- Small agent footprint

Single Console

Simplify Setup and Deployment

- Quickly and easily install & update agents
- Shared settings streamlines deployments

Endpoint Policy Enforcement

- Tracks endpoint compliance by rule
- Enforces policy for 3rd party antivirus

Unified Security Architecture

Unified Endpoint and network Security Management

- Endpoint Security logs can be monitored from SmartCenter
- Centralized security event correlation management and reporting with Eventia® Suite
- Shared management server, log-in, and console

Agenda

Endpoint Security Solution

Powerful Security

Industry-leading Firewall

15 years of Firewall Leadership

- Proactive inbound and outbound protection
- Blocks unwanted network traffic
- Stealth mode – makes endpoint invisible to hackers
- Segmentation contains outbreaks and enables high granularity network access control

Network Access Control

Ensure Endpoint Policy Compliance

- Internal and VPN NAC

- Ensures only safe PCs are allowed to access network
- Cooperative enforcement with Check Point and 3rd party gateways
- 802.1x support enables NAC in multi-vendor networking environments

Enhanced Program Control

Program Advisor Service

- Automatically terminates know malicious programs
- Immediately terminates known malicious programs
- Ensures only legitimate and approved programs run on the PC
- How do we do it?
- Known good application authenticity service
- Known bad malware identification
- Over 300,000 applications in Program Advisor database
- Based on real-time data from millions of endpoints

Antivirus / Anti-spyware

Eliminate Viruses and other Malware

- Award-winning engine delivers the best virus protection
- Highest detection rates

- Fastest antivirus / anti-malware response
- 12 hours (compared to 24-48 hours industry average)
- Hourly signature updates

Data Security

Protect Data from Loss for Traffic

- Check Point is the most widely deployed solution for protecting valuable data
- 14 million seats deployed
- Based on Pointsec® market-leading technology
- Full Disk Encryption – provides the most complete & comprehensive protection for all data
- Port Protection – keeps data safe by controlling activity on ports and devices
- Media Encryption – encrypts sensitive data transferred via portable media devices such as USB flash drives

Remote Access

Unified Remote Access

- Secure remote VPN access through VPN-1®
- Only endpoint security solution that includes unified remote access
- Applies full security policies to the VPN traffic

- Multiple VPN entry points provides high availability and flexible access

Agenda

Endpoint Security Solution

Summary

Endpoint Security Comparison

Requirements NetSec Antivirus Data Sec Check Point

Powerful Security

Firewall/NAC Program Control

Antivirus Anti-spyware

Data Security

VPN

Unified Management

Checkpoint Endpoint Security is the first single agent for total endpoint security

Summary

- **Single Agents Single Console** for Simplified Execution
- **Powerful Security** for Confident Protection

Investigative Best Practices with Threat Prevention

Introduction

Organizations today are facing unprecedented growth in the diversity and number of security threats from advanced and sophisticated malware.

To help stay ahead of modern malware,

Early detection and rapid response is essential!

Introduction

Providing easy-to-use tools and guidelines for implementing malware investigation process, using the Threat Prevention Software Blades.

Using this guide you will be able to:

Investigate if a host is truly infected with malware

Identify the malware type and potential damages

Detect suspicious behavior that might indicate additional infected computers

Remediate inflect computers

Advanced Threat Prevention

Anti-Virus

Threat Emulation

Anti-Bot

IPS

Incident Handing Process

Prepare Optimizing configuration based on network topology

Identify Monitor Threat Prevention events to identity suspicious hosts

Investigate Conclude if the host is inflected and with what type of malware and its behavior

Track Track infected computers' activity to identify additional infected computers

Remediate Remover infected machines

Preparations

Maximizing visibility

Preparations

Improve Threat Visibility

1. Prepare my SmartEvent View

2. Improve visibility when computers are behind proxy

and/or DNS server

Preparations

1. Prepare my SmartEvent View

Review Threat Preventation events grouped by Source:

1. In SmartEvent. Click Events tab

2. From the left-pane, click: predefined > Threat Prevention > All Events.

Note: Adjust presented time according to review period (default is 12H)

Periodic Monitoring with SmartEvent

Unlike log utilities, SmartEvent provides high-level overview that also lets you zero in during an analysis.

Schedule a routine to review, analyze and subsequently respond to alerts.

Preparations

2.1 Improve visibility by using XFF when computers are behind proxy server

In some network topologies, security events might seem to be triggered by the proxy server, falsely indicating that the proxy server in infected with bot, while the actual infected computers are computers deployed behind it.

If computers are behind proxy, enable X-Forward-For (XFF) on your proxy server to identify the actual infected computers

Roxy XFF (X-Forwarded-For)

Use your Proxy's feature to include the Source IP in the log.

1. Configure the Proxy to include the XFF, so the XFF will be displayed in the log.

2. You can configure the Gateway to strip the XFF field so it won't be revealed. For more information, follow SK100223.

Preparations

2.2 Improve visibility when internal DNS server is deployed by enabling 'Malware DSN Trap' feature

The issue: The Security Gateway blocks DNS requests to malicious websites. However, when an internal DNS server is deployed, the gateway will recognize the internal DNS server IP as the source of these requests indicating that the DNS server might be infected while the actual infected machine is a different computer, behind the DNS server

Solution: To identify computers generating DNS request to malicious websites when internal DNS server is deployed enable 'Malware DNS Trap' features on Security Gateway.

Identity

Hosts with Anti-Bot (AB) incidents

Severity levels Medium and above should be investigated immediately

Identify additional suspicious computer

Hosts with multiple Anti-Virus (AV) incidents

Any severity, also when event Severity is Low…

Detect mode incidents

Anti-Virus (AV) or Threat Emulation (TE) incidents in detect mode.

If the incident was identified but was not blocked due to detection mode configuration, further investigate if the machine got infected

Other Threat Prevention incidents

The suspicious computers detected so far should be treated with high priority. However, if there are additional security events related to computers that are not a part of the list of computers flagged in the previous steps, these additional computers can be treated with lower priority (using the same investigation methodology described in the following sections).

Investigate

Investigate

Investigate a suspicious computer

- Investigate suspicious computers in order to: conclude if the computers infected (is it real?) cleaning an infected computer might consume a lot of time and resources. To maximize efficiency, there is a need to identify computers that are infected with high confidence.
- Determine malware type (what is it?) In addition it is also important to identify the malware type in order to decide the right cleaning method.

Investigate

Investigate a suspicious computer

After identifying suspicious computers, now it is time to investigate the incidents following 3 steps:

- Correlating events
- Deep-dive Analysis
- Suspicious indicators

Investigate

1. Correlating events

When correlating multiple Threat Prevention events, observe the following:

1.1 Events with different protection types

1.2 Events with different protection names

1.3 Suspicious Anti-Virus Events

Event Correlation

1.1 Events with different protection types

Anti-Bot uses several protection types:

1.1 Events with different protection

If a computer triggered AB incidents of two different Protection Types*, you can conclude that the host is infected with high confidence.

*note that protection types from two different categories indicates stronger confidence (e.g. IP reputation and Signature)

Event Correlation

The Protection Name reflects the indicator (e.g. URL, IP, pattern) which was used to detect the infection.

Each protection triggered on the host is further evidence of possible infection, thus increasing the assurance it is infected.

Event Correlation

1.3 Suspicious Anti-Virus Events

Indications that Anti-Virus events are actually Bot actions:

- Anti-Virus events followed by Anti-Bot events
- Multiple reputation events
- Suspicious Patters
- Time pattern
- Repeating incidents

Investigate

2. Drill-down Event Analysis

Use the following tools and guidelines to gather more information about a single event:

2.1 Confidence Level

2.2 Connection Scope

2.3 Address Analysis

2.4 Event Time

2.5 ThreatWiki

2.6 Malware Analysis

Drill-down Event Analysis

2.1 Confidence Level

The higher the confidence level is the more chances that the event is triggered by a real bot or AV incident.

Confidence level indicates how confident the Software Blade is that recognized attacks are actually virus or bot traffic. Some attack types are more subtle than others and legitimate traffic can sometimes be mistakenly recognized as a threat. The confidence level value shows how well protections can correctly recognize a specific attack.

Drill-down Event Analysis

2.2 Connection Scope

Check the Source / Destination – which hosts are involved?

AB incidents will be triggered primarily on outgoing connections. However, consider these exceptions:

Drill-down Event Analysis

2.3 Address Analusis

Review and analyze the Destination / Resource field.

Signs that an address is malicious:

A. Unusual destination country

B. 'Fishy' Domain names

C. Randomized Domain names

D. Multiple destination addresses in the log

E. 'whois' shows suspicious info

F. Low reputation according to 3rd party engines

G. Low popularity using Google search

Address Analysis

A. Destination Country

Check the location of the external resource i.e. Destination Country

Is this traffic typical for your organization?

Address Analysis

B. 'Fishy' Domain name (typosquatting)

Common service that is misspelled. For example:

'windows'

'hotmeil'

'windows.cc'

Address Analysis

C. Randomized Domain names

Check if the URL looks as if it was create by a DGA. In most cases you will notice multiple AB or AV reputation incidents over a short time frame (Bot callback)

Address Analysis

D. Multiple destinations in the event itself

A single protection triggered over multiple connections

- P2P connections to multiple Bots
- HTTP connection to a malicious Domain but different paths

Address Analysis

E. Suspicious registration/status info using 'whois'

Go to whois.domaintools.com to get more info about the URL or IP.

- (IP) organization name and contacts
- (IP, URL) Server status: Is it inactive?
- (URL) Registration: Is the Domain registered? Only recently?

- (URL) The Domain is for sale.

Address Analysis

F. External reputation engines

It is also recommended to use free web reputation services such as: Virustotal.com and mywot.com.

Address Analysis

G. Site popularity

Check popularity of the Domain

- Google the Domain and check number of the results
- Use analysis engines (e.g. Alexa.com) and check it's report

Address Analysis

To understand how analysis of the destination address impact the confidence that the host is indeed infected, consider the Protection Type:

- Anti-Bot Network Patters: address is independent. In most cases it will not be recognized yet by 3rd party reputation engines since the detection is by pattern.

Address Analysis – Guidelines

- Reputation-based: analyze the address to validate

- For some specific types of bot activities, the destination address will be legitimate:
- P2P communications
- Bot connectivity testing
- Suspicious Mail

Drill-down Event Analysis

2.4 Event Time

Check the Time of the event

Is it usual for your organization's working hours?

Drill-down Event Analysis

2.5 ThreatWiki

Search the Protection Name in the ThreatWiki tool: threatwiki.checkpoint.com.

This tool queries the ThreatCloud database and provides more information about threats and its classification.

ThreatWiki

Go to threatWiki.checkpoint.com and search the protection name:

ThreatWiki

You can also navigate directly from the event card in

SmatEvent:

ThreatWiki

The information presented will help you to learn more about the threat

ThreatWiki

Malware Naming Convention

Check Point, as most security vendors, uses this convention to define malware.

Type: Classifies the threat behavior (Throjan, Virus, Adware, Backdoor)

Platform: The operating system on which the threat works (Win32, DOS)

Family: Classification according to similarities in the code, or origin.

Variant: Malware version, or any differentiation that results in different hash

ThreatWiki

Risk Level

Classifies Risk level of threats:

(5) – (4) **Critical** and **High**: Malware and Malicious tools

with high or critical risk for potential damage.

(3) **Medium**: Pornware or other Riskware, as well as non-recent malware.

(2) **Low**: Adware – Unwanted software that display advertisements, but can also send information about the user.

(1) **Very Low**: "not-a-virus" – Risky but legal software that can be used by criminals for compromising users.

ThreatWiki

Malware Family

> ➢ Click on the <u>Malware Family name</u> to read more about this family.
> For common family names, ThreatWiki includes generic entries with extended information.
> ➢ The <u>first line in the description</u> will specify additional names for this family, if exists.

ThreatWiki

Obsolete Records

In case the Protection has been removed from the ThreatCloud database, there would be a statement that this protection is obsolete.

Drill-down Event Analysis

2.6 Malware Analysis

In case of a virus incident, further investigate the type of virus detected in order to understand the risk.

- A. **Study Threat Emulation Reports**: This will also help you to conclude whether the user machine is infected.
- B. **Cross-reference the file hash**

Malware Analysis

A. study Threat Emulation Reports

- What URLs have been accessed by the TE VM machine?
- Check if the user accessed these URLs:
- Go to SmartLog search and type: "malicious_address"
- If the user accessed these URL, it means it is infected
- What Processes have been opened?
- Check using our EP Compliance Blade!

Malware Analysis

B. Cross-reference the file hash

Use VirusTotal to find more information about the threat:

1. Go to www.virustotal.com
2. Chose "Search" and enter the file hash

3. A report will be presented with info about the threat.

Investigate

2. Drill-down Analysis – Summary

Investigate

2. Suspicious Indicators

If URL Filtering and Application Control are enabled, search for additional unusual behavior from the host in question. This will help to validate whether the host is indeed infected.

Pay close attention to the following:

3.1 Malicious URLs

3.2 Direct Requests to the Internet

Suspicious Indicators

3.1 Malicious URLs

Perform historical analysis to identify additional connections to infected sites.

- Review HTTP/S outgoing connections and look for suspicious URLs.
- Investigate according to analysis guidelines 2.3
- List all suspicious addresses you have identified

Malicious URLs

- In below example, the administrator would like to perform additional checks to confirm the infection.
- We will sure SmartEvent to analyze the URLs the user accessed around the time of the below incidents

Malicious URLs

To review all sites the host has accessed, shortly by time:

1. In SmartEvent, click the Events tab
2. From the lefi-pane, click: Predefined > APCL & URLF > More > Sites
3. On the upper right choose > Group by Source
4. Right click on Source > Edit Filter and add the suspicious IP
5. Sort by Start Rime and scroll to the relevant time

Malicious URLs

Focus on the following:

1. URLF alerts

2. Category field:

   a) General
   b) High Risk
   c) In-active

3. Suspicious Countries

4. Unusual working hours

Suspicious Indicators

3.2 Direct Requests to the Internet

It is common for malware to send constructed packets that will try to bypass the local servers.

Review outgoing connections from the host (including FW drops) and search for direct requests to external Internet addresses, such as:

- Clients not using DNS servers
- HTTP connections not via Proxy

Investigate

Summary

- Correlating events
- Deep-dive Analysis
- Suspicious Indicators

Track

Track infected computers' activity to trace additional infections on network

Review

Identify Additional Infections

When validating infections, as shown in the previous stage (Investigate), use these new finding to trace additional infections in your network:

1. Classify Related Events

2. Review Traffic to Malicious Addresses

Review

1. Classify Related Events

After confirming infections, look for repeating events on other hosts:

1. In SmartEvent view, group events by Protection Name

3. Classify as infected hosts with the same confirmed incidents

3. Investigate hosts with events of similar malware family

Classify Related Events

It is recommended to use the SmartEvent Ticketing feature in order to keep track of past investigations

Review

2. Review Traffic to Malicious Addresses

- List all suspicious addresses you have identified during the investigation phase conducted previously:
- These are all the malicious or unknown destination addresses seen from the infected host.
- Investigation all machines that have been communicating with these addresses. These machines are likely to be infected.

Review Traffic to Malicious Addresses

Review all outbound activity to malicious addresses you have identified:

1. Open SmartLog

2. Go to quick search and type: dst: <malicious_address>

Remediate

Remediate

Remediation Procedure

1. Isolate

2. Computer Classification

3. Consider Remediation Tools

4. Re-image

5. Recover

6. Increase Awareness

Remediation Procedure

1. Isolate

Disconnect the computer from the network and notify the user that the computer cannot be re-connected until all malware has been successfully removed.

Remediation Procedure

2. Computer Classification

Study the malware before proceeding with remediation (as shown in 'Investigate' phase).

What is the malware family and it's primary purpose?

- AB log should include it
- Search the Web for aliases

Remediation Procedure

3. Consider Remediation Tools

- If it is possible to identify the malware installed, use dedicated remediation utilities
- You can find a list of tools on the Check Point website

Remediation Procedure

4. Re-image

- It is always recommended to re-image an infected machine to ensure that it is completely free of malware.
- Also notice that malware can remove itself from the machine when it detects that a malware removal tool is running

Remediation Procedure

5. Recover

- Change any default passwords (e.g. local admin passwords and certificates). These are precisely the types of credentials the bot will aim to acquire.
- If possible, consider remediating all infected machined at the same time. Otherwise, other infected hosts could begin to re-infect (the previously cleaned hosts using stolen credentials.

Remediation Procedure

6. Increase Awareness

Following the incident, awareness should be increased to identify re-occurrence infections.

Summary

Identity

Improve Visibility to detect infections al early stage:

- Use SmartEvent
- PerformPeriodic Monitoring
- ConsiderYour Topology

Investigate

Conclude if the hosts infected:

- Correlate events on the host
- Drill-down Event for each event
- Look for suspicious indicators

Review

Use past finding to identify new infection:

- Classify related events
- Who communicated with the malicious addresses?

Remediate

- Recover the infected machine.
- Re-image if possible.